FACT FINDERS ANIMALS

FISH

Izzi Howell

WINDMILL BOOKS

Published in 2018 by **Windmill Books**, an Imprint of Rosen Publishing
29 East 21ˢᵗ Street, New York, NY 10010

Editor: Izzi Howell
Design: Clare Nicholas
Other illustrations: Stefan Chabluk
Consultant: Kate Ruttle

Picture and illustration credits: Corbis: David Shale/Nature Picture Library 21; iStock: qldian title page, tingfen 4tl, qldian 4bl, viridis 5, strmko 6, ifish 9, renacali 17, Whitepointer 18; Shutterstock: iliuta goean cover, frantisekhojdysz 4tr, Songsak Pandet 4br, Mirko Rosenau 7t, Hayati Kayhan 7b, LauraD 8, Filip Fuxa 10t, stockpix4u 10b, Richard Whitcombe 11, Rich Carey 12, Amanda Nicholls 13, Levent Konuk 14, Rich Carey 15 and 16, Peter Leahy 19, Beth Swanson 20.

Cataloging-in-Publication Data
Names: Howell, Izzi.
Title: Fish / Izzi Howell.
Description: New York : Windmill Books, 2017. Series: Fact finders: animals Includes index.
Identifiers: ISBN 9781499483079 (pbk.) ISBN 9781499483024 (library bound) ISBN 9781499482935 (6 pack)
Subjects: LCSH: Fishes--Juvenile literature.
Classification: LCC QL617.2 H69 2017 DDC 597--dc23

Manufactured in China
CPSIA Compliance Information: Batch #BS17WM: For Further Information contact
Rosen Publishing, New York, New York at 1-800-237-9932

FACT FINDER

There is a question for you to answer on each spread in this book. You can check your answers on page 24.

CONTENTS

WHAT IS A FISH?

Fish are a group of animals that are similar to each other in certain ways. Fish live underwater and breathe using **gills**. Most fish are covered in **scales**.

Leafy sea dragons, hammerhead sharks, eagle rays, and koi carp are all types of fish.

leafy sea dragon

hammerhead shark

eagle ray

koi carp

Almost all fish are **cold-blooded**. Cold-blooded animals can't control the temperature of their bodies. They have a high temperature in warm water, and a low temperature in cold water.

Butterfly fish need to stay warm to **survive** so they live in **tropical** seas and oceans.

FACT FINDER

Although jellyfish and starfish have the word "fish" in their name, they are not fish. This is because fish have **backbones**, but jellyfish and starfish do not. Can you find out another animal with "fish" in its name that isn't a fish?

HABITAT

Some fish live in the **salt water** of seas and oceans. Many of the fish that we eat, such as cod and mackerel, come from **temperate** and **polar** oceans.

FACT FINDER

Bull sharks and river sharks can live in both salt water and freshwater. In South America, bull sharks have been found in rivers that are thousands of miles (kilometers) from the sea!

Most sharks, such as this gray reef shark, live in salt water.

Many fish live in **freshwater** lakes and rivers. Some freshwater fish are very large, such as the 400-pound (180 kg) arapaima. Others are small, such as neon tetras, which are only 1 inch (2.5 cm) long.

neon tetra

Shoals of red-bellied piranhas swim together in the lakes and rivers of South America. What do red-bellied piranhas eat?

BREATHING

Like all animals, fish need **oxygen** to survive. Instead of getting oxygen from the air as humans do, almost all fish get oxygen from water.

Most fish, like this lionfish, need water to breathe.

As water passes through a fish's body, its gills take oxygen from the water. Then, the fish's gills open to let the water flow out of its body.

A fish's gills are on the side of its head.

gills

FACT FINDER

The lungfish takes in oxygen from the air as well as from water. Lungfish can leave the water and live on land in mud **burrows**. Can you find out another fish that can live out of water?

SKIN

Fish have different kinds of scales. Most fish are covered in large, smooth scales, but sharks and rays have small, hard scales.

Shark skin is so rough that other animals can get hurt if they touch it.

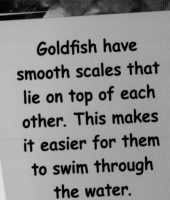

Goldfish have smooth scales that lie on top of each other. This makes it easier for them to swim through the water.

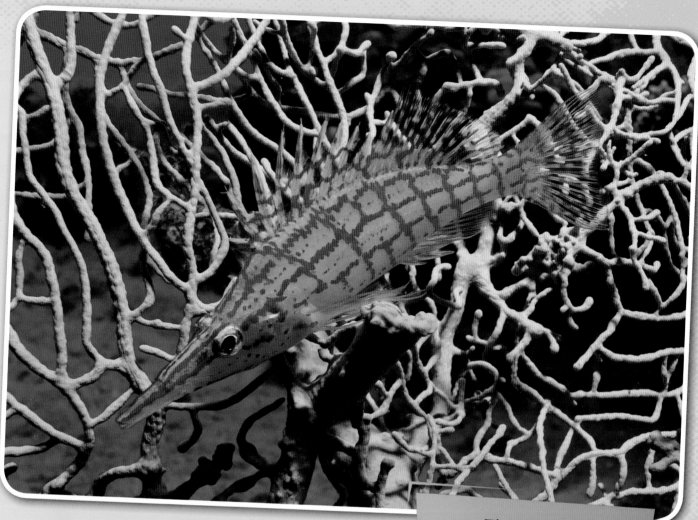

The color of a fish's scales can help it to hide from **predators**. Fish that live far from the **coast** are often blue or black so that they match the color of the deep water.

The longnose hawkfish has a striped pattern which looks like the **coral reef** where it lives.

FACT FINDER

The cleaner wrasse fish cleans the skin of other fish! How does it do this?

DIET

Many fish are **carnivores**. They have sharp teeth that help them to catch and eat other animals for food.

The strong teeth of this titan triggerfish can break through the hard shells of **shellfish**, such as crabs.

The whale shark only eats plankton. It uses the **filter** in its mouth to take plankton out of the water.

Many freshwater and saltwater fish eat **plankton**. Plankton are extremely small animals and plants that live in water. Fish that eat plankton are **omnivores**, because they eat both plants and animals.

FACT FINDER

Whale sharks are the largest fish on Earth. They are up to 40 feet (12 m) long, which is longer than a bus! How much do you think a whale shark weighs?

YOUNG

Most fish **young** are born from eggs. **Female** fish lay their eggs in the water.

This clown fish has laid its eggs on the side of a rock.

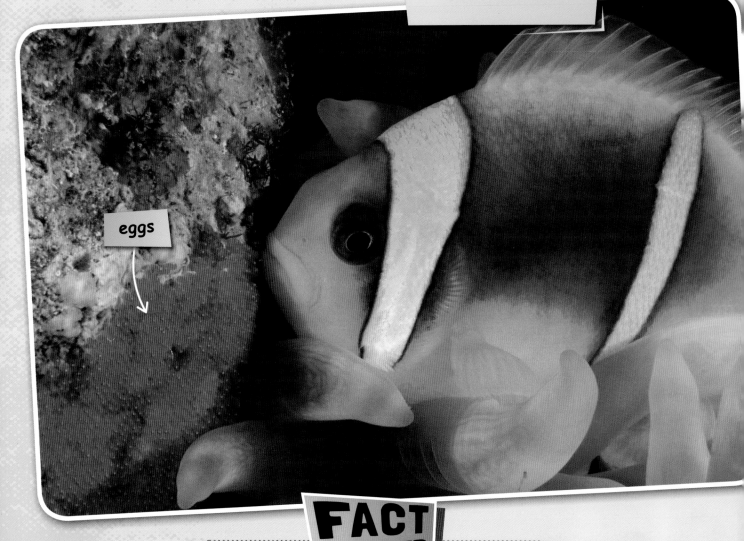

eggs

FACT FINDER

The eggs of the sturgeon fish are one of the most expensive foods in the world. What is another name for this dish?

Some female fish leave their eggs to hatch on their own. Other fish stay with their eggs and take care of their young after they are born.

Many sharks give birth to live young. This whitetip reef shark was born ready to look after itself.

MOVEMENT

Most fish swim by moving their body and tail in an "s" shape. This movement pushes them forwards through the water.

This bigeye fish uses its **fins** to move up and down in the water.

Not all fish move in the same way. Rays move through the water by flapping their fins. Eels use the muscles in their long bodies to swim forwards, just as a snake moves across land.

Manta rays can jump out of the water for a few seconds.

SENSES

One of the most important senses for fish is sight. Most fish can see well from far away and recognize different colors.

This great white shark smells through holes in its nose called nostrils. Most sharks have an excellent sense of smell.

nostril

FACT FINDER

Great white sharks can smell blood in the water from 3 miles (5 km) away! Are great white sharks **herbivores**, carnivores or omnivores?

lateral
line

The **lateral line** along the side of a fish's body can sense movement and sound in the water. This lets fish know if there is a predator nearby.

The lateral line of this Spanish hogfish starts from its eye and ends by its tail.

STRANGE FISH

When the puffer fish senses danger, it swallows a lot of water. The extra water in its body makes it grow much bigger, which means that predators won't want to eat it.

This puffer fish has spines on its skin that stick out when it puffs up.

FACT FINDER

If a predator eats a puffer fish, it is likely that the predator will die. Puffer fish are one of the most poisonous animals on Earth!

There isn't much light down in the deep ocean. Some deep ocean fish make their own light to bring **prey** towards them.

The female anglerfish has a light hanging off its head. How did the anglerfish get its name?

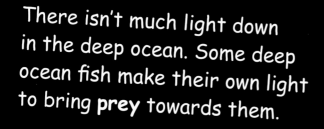

QUIZ

Try to answer the questions below. Look back through the book to help you. Check your answers on page 24.

1 Starfish are fish. True or not true?

a) true

b) not true

2 Where do red-bellied piranhas live?

a) Africa

b) Europe

c) South America

3 Almost all fish get oxygen from water. True or not true?

a) true

b) not true

4 What do carnivores eat?

a) plants

b) other animals

c) plants and other animals

5 Female fish lay their eggs out of the water. True or not true?

a) true

b) not true

6 Which of these fish is poisonous?

a) puffer fish

b) anglerfish

c) clown fish

GLOSSARY

backbone the line of bones down the center of the back

burrow a hole that an animal digs in the ground to live in

carnivore an animal that only eats meat

coast the area of land that is next to the ocean

cold-blooded describes an animal whose body temperature depends on the temperature of its surroundings

coral reef a tropical sea habitat made from coral

female an animal that can get pregnant and give birth to young

filter something that you use to take a solid out of a liquid

fin a thin part of a fish's body that is used to help it move through water

freshwater water that does not contain salt and is found in lakes or rivers

gill a part of the body that fish breathe through

herbivore an animal that only eats plants

lateral line a line along the side of a fish's body that helps it to sense movement

omnivore an animal that eats plants and meat

oxygen a gas in the air that animals need to breathe to live

plankton very small plants and animals that live in the ocean and are eaten by other animals

polar describes an ocean with cold water

predator an animal that kills and eats other animals

prey an animal that is killed and eaten by other animals

salt water water that contains salt and is found in the sea or ocean

scales small pieces of hard skin that cover the bodies of fish

shellfish sea animals that have a hard outer shell for a body

shoal a large group of fish that swim together

survive to stay alive and not die

temperate describes an ocean with some warm and some cold water

tropical describes an ocean with warm water

young an animal's babies

INDEX

ANSWERS

Pages 4–21

Page 5: Starfish and cuttlefish aren't fish even though they have the word "fish" in their names.

Page 7: Red-bellied piranhas eat fish, insects, and plants.

Page 9: Mudskippers and some eels can live out of water.

Page 11: The cleaner wrasse fish eats the dead skin of other fish.

Page 13: Whale sharks can weigh about 21 tons (19mt)!

Page 14: Caviar

Page 17: Tuna, swordfish, and other large fish eat flying fish.

Page 18: Sharks are carnivores.

Page 21: "Angler" is another word for fisherman. Anglerfish catch their prey like fishermen using fishing poles.

Quiz answers

1   not true – they do not have backbones.

2   c - South America

3   true

4   b – other animals

5   not true – they lay their eggs in the water.

6   a – puffer fish